SIGNATURE MOVES

THE FINISHING MOVES OF SPORT ENTERTAINMENT SUPERSTARS

World
Wrestling
Entertainment®
BOOKS

There was no powering out of a

CHOKEHOLD

applied by the seven-foot-four,
five-hundred-and-twenty-pound

"EIGHTH WONDER OF THE WORLD,"

ANDRE
THE GIANT!

REY MYSTERIO DIALS UP THE "619," ON ORLANDO JORDAN!

AREA CODE OF HIS NATIVE SAN DIEGO, NAMING HIS MODIFIED TIGER FEINT KICK THROUGH THE ROPES AFTER THE

WWE HALL OF FAME

SUPERSTAR "MR. WONDERFUL"

PAUL
ORNDORFF

STRONG-ARMED MANY

OPPONENTS BEFORE DRIVING

THEM DOWN HEADFIRST

WITH A THUNDEROUS

PILEDRIVER.

A SMUG **RENE DUPREE** PREMATURELY CELEBRATES IN THE RING WITH HIS ARROGANT SIDESTEP, THE **FRENCH TICKLER.**

"ROWDY"

RODDY

PIPER

won the Intercontinental title, his only **WWE** championship, at *Royal Rumble 1992*, after placing the Mountie in his renowned

SLEEPER

HOLD.

The Great One,

THE ROCK,

PREPARES TO

ELECTRIFY

the crowd in Toronto's Skydome—and Hollywood Hogan—with the

PEOPLE'S ELBOW

at *WrestleMania X8!*

DELIVERS A ROUNDHOUSE
CHICK
KICK
TO VICTORIA!

DIVAS GONE WILD:
TRISH STRATUS

THE TEXAS
RATTLESNAKE,
STONE COLD
STEVE AUSTIN,
ADDED VENOM
TO THE
LOU THESZ
PRESS
BY QUICKLY
PUMMELING
AWAY AT THE
ADVERSARIES HE
BOWLED OVER.

HULKAMANIA RUNS WILD AS THE IMMORTAL HULK HOGAN FOLLOWS UP A BIG BOOT TO THE FACE WITH A CRUSHING LEGDROP!

GREGORY HELMS

WHACKS NUNZIO WITH HIS HURRICANE-FORCE ENZUIGIRI KICK, THE SHINING WIZARD!

"RAVISHING" RICK RUDE

DELIVERED A HANGMAN'S NECKBREAKER THAT WAS MORE THAN A "RUDE AWAKENING" FOR ANYONE CAUGHT IN THE HOLD.

BRUTUS "THE BARBER" BEEFCAKE

WEARS DOWN GREG "THE HAMMER" VALENTINE IN THE

BARBER'S CHAIR,

HIS CUTTING-EDGE SLEEPER HOLD.

IT'S NOT A PRETTY PICTURE
FOR ANYONE CAUGHT IN
MNM'S
FLAPJACK DDT, THE
SNAPSHOT!

CHRIS MASTERS

CLAMPS DOWN
ON JOHN CENA WITH HIS
UNBREAKABLE
FULL NELSON, THE
MASTER LOCK

BUSHWACKERS

Butch and Luke entertained WWE fans around the world, but

PUNISHED

their ring opposition with the

DOUBLE
GUT BUSTER.

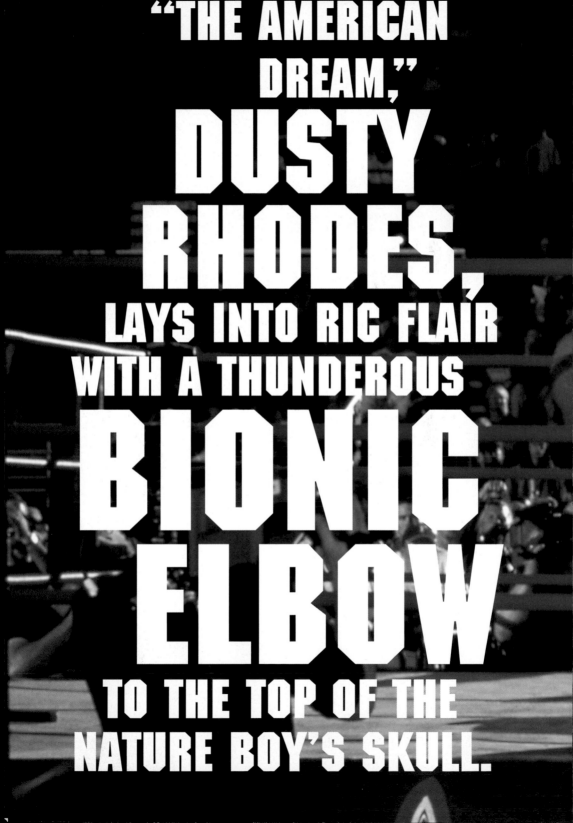

"THE AMERICAN DREAM," **DUSTY RHODES,** LAYS INTO RIC FLAIR WITH A THUNDEROUS **BIONIC ELBOW** TO THE TOP OF THE NATURE BOY'S SKULL.

MICKIE JAMES **GETS READY TO DELIVER SOME** STRATUSFACTION **TO THE DIVA WHO INVENTED THE TOP-ROPE BULLDOG, TRISH STRATUS.**

STRATUSFACTION

WILLIAM REGAL

fancies himself a distinguished Englishman, but relies on **"THE POWER OF THE PUNCH"** to finish off adversaries like Scotty 2 Hotty.

SGT. SLAUGHTER—

A NAME HE EARNED BACK IN THE U.S. MARINE CORPS—FORCES ANOTHER MAGGOT TO **SURRENDER** TO HIS INESCAPABLE SLEEPER HOLD, THE

COBRA
CLUTCH!

to the Heartbreak Kid,
SHAWN MICHAELS!

Superkicking the Big
Show's skull sounds like
SWEET CHIN
MUSIC

JOHN "BRADSHAW" LAYFIELD FINISHES HOLLY OFF WITH AN EXPLOSIVE CLOTHESLINE FROM HELL!

Even Hulk Hogan was HARD-PRESSED to withstand the disastrous IMPACT of a 460-pound EARTHQUAKE SPLASH!

EVERYBODY HAD A PRICE FOR "THE MILLION DOLLAR MAN" TED DiBIASE, OR ELSE THEY PAID THE PRICE IN HIS SLEEPER HOLD, THE MILLION DOLLAR DREAM.

TORRIE WILSON

literally

DOGS

Candice Michelle

with a

CHLOE TUSH PUSH

during their Playboy Pillow Fight at *WrestleMania 22.*

EDGE NEARLY SPEARS VAL VENIS IN HALF, DRIVING THE RATED R SUPERSTAR TO ANOTHER RAW WIN.

HARDCORE LEGEND MICK FOLEY AND "MR. SOCKO" LEAVE A BITTER TASTE IN THE TRASH-TALKING MOUTH OF RANDY ORTON.

SIGNATURE MOVES

IN YOUR

FACE

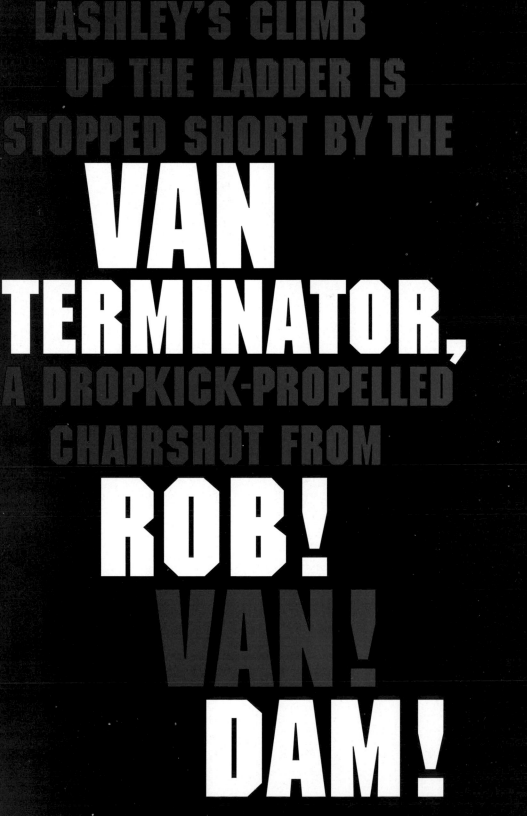

DIVA POWERHOUSE VICTORIA

STRIKES AGAIN WITH HER ELEVATED SHOULDER NECKBREAKER, THE **WIDOW'S PEAK**.

AN EFFORTLESS GORILLA-PRESS SLAM, FOLLOWED BY AN AWESOME RUNNING SPLASH, RESULTED IN MANY DECISIVE VICTORIES FOR THE HIGH-OCTANE ULTIMATE WARRIOR!

RENE DUPREE RESTS IN PEACE AFTER A MONSTROUS CHOKESLAM FROM UNDERTAKER.

A FACE-CRUSHER TO THE CANVAS SETS JOEY MERCURY UP FOR THE FOREARM CHOP

SCOTTY 2 HOTTY SPELLS W-O-R-M!

THE **BIG BOSS MAN** METED OUT HIS OWN BRAND OF **LAW ENFORCEMENT** THROUGHOUT WWE WITH HIS SPINNING POWERSLAM, THE **BOSS MAN SLAM!**

THE ROCK

"layeth the smacketh down" with a

ROCK BOTTOM

sideslam on Stone Cold Steve Austin at *WrestleMania XV.*

AT *WrestleMania 21,* "LEGEND KILLER" RANDY ORTON TRIES ENDING UNDERTAKER'S UNDEFEATED *WrestleMania* RECORD WITH HIS INVERTED NECKBREAKER, THE RKO!

JEFF HARDY

redefines "HIGH-RISK MANEUVER" at *WrestleMania XVI*, hitting Bubba Ray Dudley with a

SWANTON BOMB

off the top of a ladder!

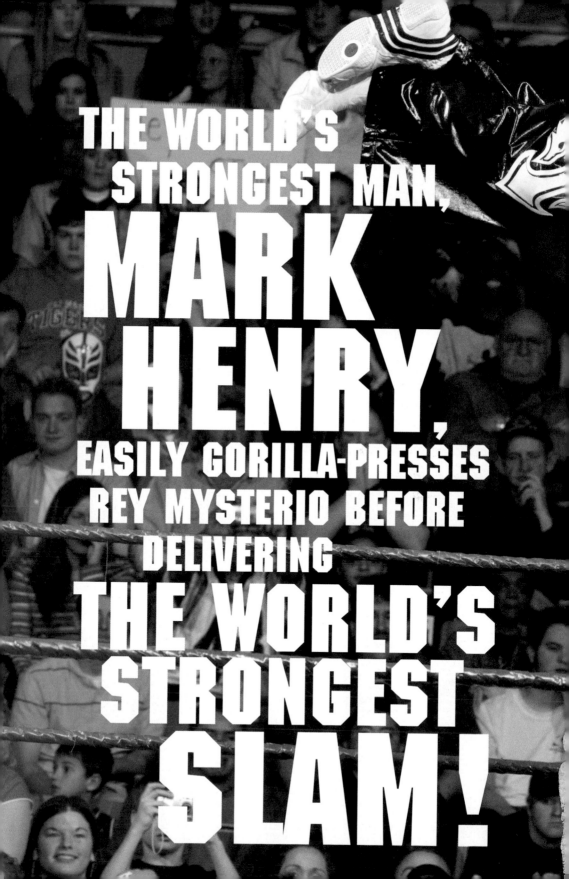

THE WORLD'S STRONGEST MAN, **MARK HENRY**, EASILY GORILLA-PRESSES REY MYSTERIO BEFORE DELIVERING **THE WORLD'S STRONGEST SLAM!**

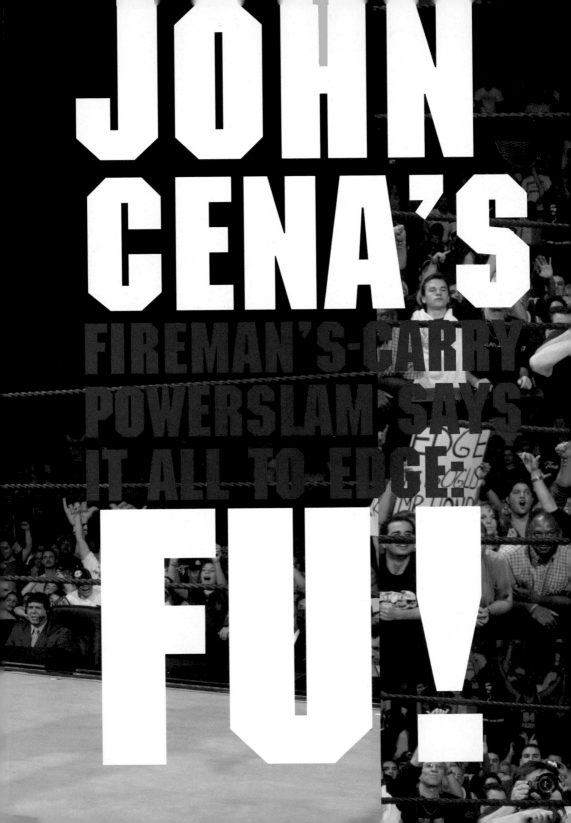

While decimating the *SmackDown!* roster at *Survivor Series 2005,* UNDERTAKER sends William Regal straight to hell with a devastating TOMBSTONE PILEDRIVER!

LASHLEY

takes charge at *Royal Rumble 2006* with his inverted front powerslam,

THE DOMINATOR!

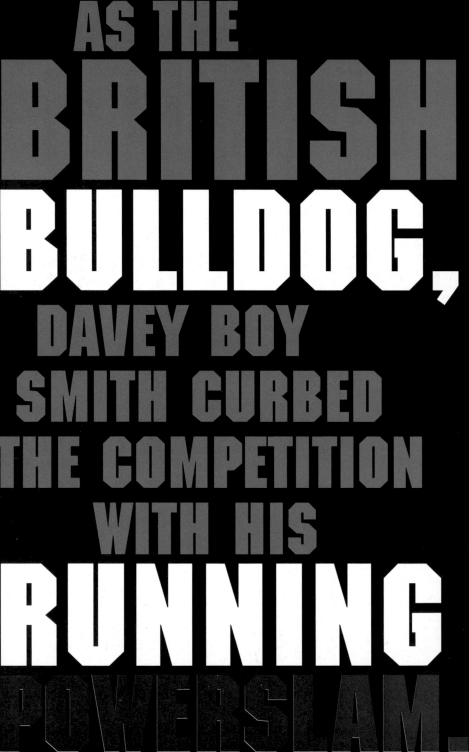

AS THE **BRITISH** **BULLDOG,** DAVEY BOY SMITH CURBED THE COMPETITION WITH HIS **RUNNING** POWERSLAM.

NOTHING
is impossible
from this
Angle—not
even an
ANGLE
SLAM
against the 400-pound
Mark Henry!

THE BIG RED
MONSTER

KANE

NEARLY
CHOKESLAMS
CARLITO
THROUGH
THE RING AT
WRESTLEMANIA 22!

BOOKER T's BOOK-END

SIDESLAM CUTS BIG SHOW DOWN TO SIZE. **CAN YOU DIG IT, SUCKA!**

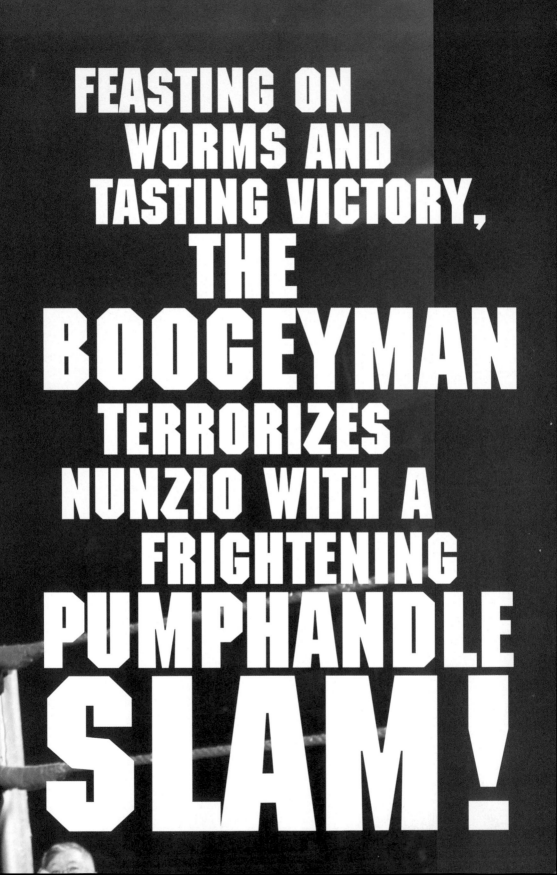

TAKING ROB VAN DAM BELLY-TO-BELLY, **SHELTON BENJAMIN** SERVES UP HIS EXPLOSIVE **T-BONE SUPLEX!**

In their Last Man Standing match at *Unforgiven 2003,* **SHANE McMAHON** takes a forty-foot **LEAP OF FAITH** off the TitanTron monitor to slay the monster Kane!

SIGNATURE MOVES

IN THE

AIR

VAL VENIS'S MATCH COMES TO AN EXCITING CLIMAX WITH HIS SPLASH FINISHER, THE MONEY SHOT!

The
always-ornery
TREVOR
MURDOCH
steers his way
to another
impressive
win with a
TOP-ROPE
BULLDOG.

LITA SHOWS OFF HER XTREME SIDE WITH A PERFECTLY EXECUTED AERIAL **MOONSAULT!**

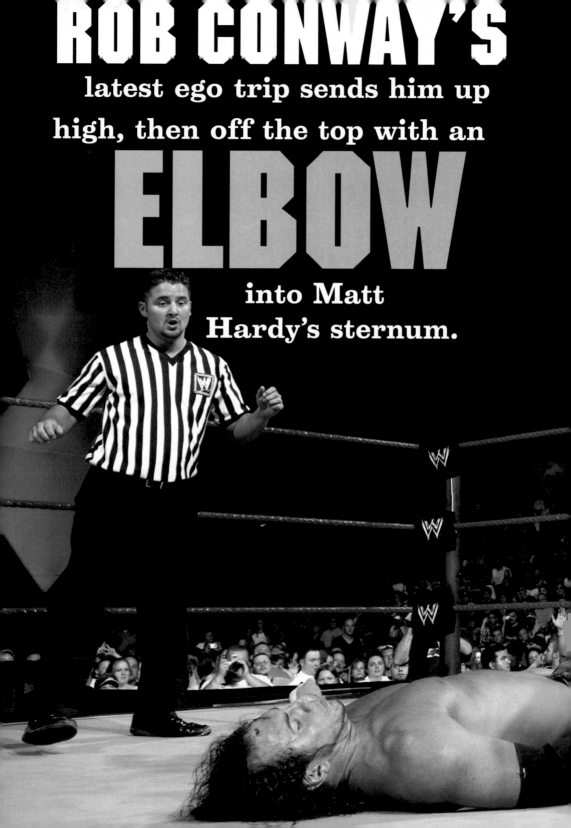

ROB CONWAY'S latest ego trip sends him up high, then off the top with an **ELBOW** into Matt Hardy's sternum.

SPRINGBOARDING OFF MARTY JANNETTY'S SHOULDERS, SHAWN MICHAELS CONNECTS WITH THE FLYING FIST DROP, JUST ONE OF SEVERAL HIGH-RISK MOVES THAT ELEVATED THE ROCKERS TO THE TOP OF WWE'S TAG-TEAM DIVISION.

KENNY

of the Spirit Squad gives John Cena little to cheer about after a punishing

TOP-ROPE

LEGDROP!

RANDY "MACHO MAN" SAVAGE

defies gravity to drop the

FLYING ELBOW

on top of Hulk Hogan
at *WrestleMania V.*

The **DOOMSDAY DEVICE**—Hawk's top-rope clothesline on opponents sitting helplessly on Animal's shoulders—cemented the **ROAD WARRIORS'** status as one of the greatest tag teams in wrestling history.

AN AIRBORNE
ROB
VAN DAM
SHUTS DOWN THE
BIG SHOW WITH THE
FIVE-STAR
FROG
SPLASH!

AND
DELIVERING
A MORTAL
BLOW
TO THE
"WRESTLING
GOD!"

UNDERTAKER GOES "OLD SCHOOL"

ON JBL, WALKING ACROSS THE TOP ROPE

WWE legend **JIMMY "SUPERFLY" SNUKA** elevated a generation of high-flying Superstars with his cross-body pinning maneuver, the

SUPERFLY SPLASH!

Ken Kennedy—
KENNEDY!
—rolls on to
victory with a
FIREMAN'S-
CARRY
SLAM
off the middle rope.

PERFORMED HIS
HIGH-FLYING

FROG SPLASH!

"LATINO HEAT"

WAS IN THE AIR WHENEVER

EDDIE GUERRERO

MEXICAN HIGH-FLYER
SUPER CRAZY
soars to victory with a
MOONSAULT
OFF THE TOP ROPE!

REY MYSTERIO

SPRINGS OFF THE ROPES, SETTING UP AN OFF-BALANCE KEN KENNEDY FOR HIS CRUSHING WEST COAST POP!

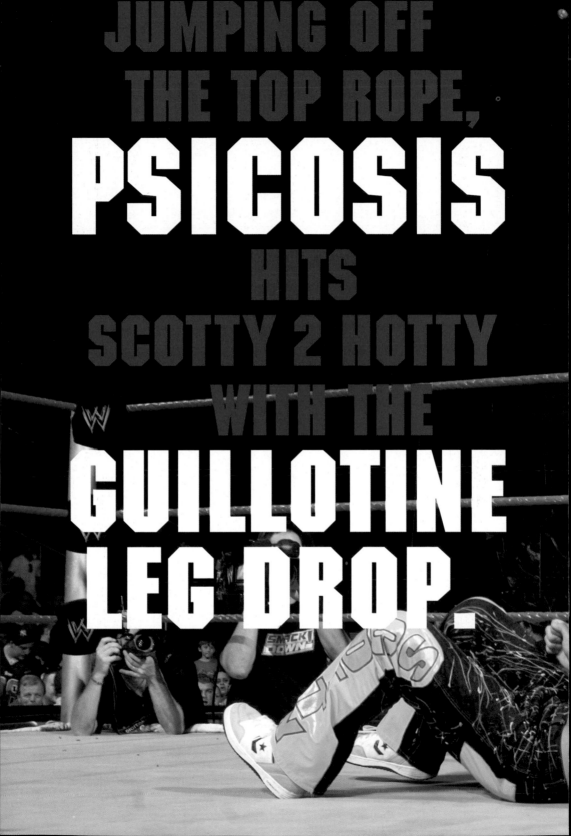

SIGNATURE MOVES

OFF THE

ROPES

HOISTING CHRIS BENOIT OVER HIS SHOULDERS, **FINLAY** PUTS THE RABID WOLVERINE DOWN WITH HIS PUNISHING BACK-TO-BELLY PILEDRIVER, THE **CELTIC CROSS!**

choking out the
gold medalist with the

TAZZMISSION

—a variation of the judo
single-wing chokehold
katahajime—at
*Royal Rumble
2000.*

TAZZ

became the first
WWE Superstar to defeat
Kurt Angle after

give the monster
a paralyzing
BACK CRACKER!

CARLITO

catches Kane with a rear chinlock, then lifts his knees and drops backward to

AN UNFORTUNATE "TWIST OF FATE" FOR CHRIS MASTERS.

MATT HARDY'S
MODIFIED SWINGING
NECKBREAKER IS

No one could
grapevine an opponent's
legs and lock on the

SHARPSHOOTER

crowned opponents with his **SPIKE PILEDRIVER.**

Before he provided color commentary on _Raw_, JERRY "THE KING" LAWLER

IT'S A LONG WAY DOWN FOR

TRIPLE H,

WHO'S ON THE RECEIVING END OF A **SPINE-JARRING CHOKESLAM** FROM THE SEVEN-FOOT, 500-POUND

BIG SHOW!

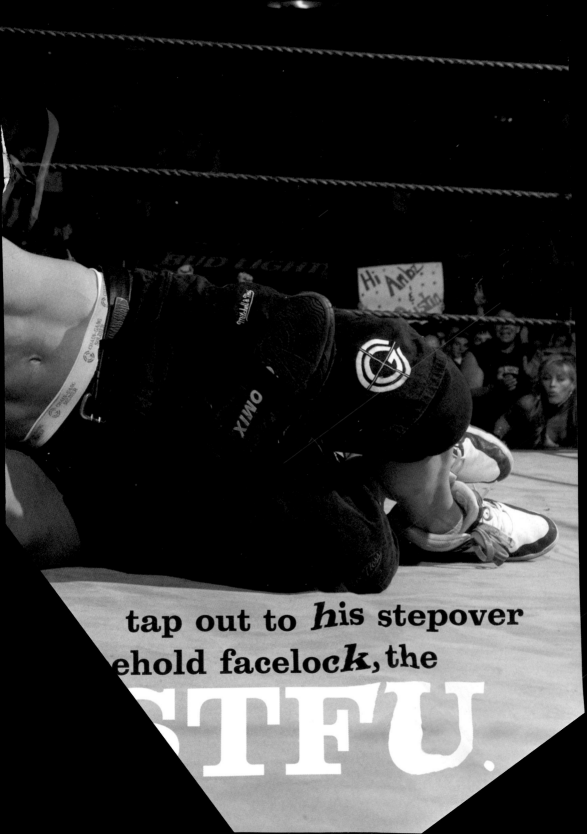

tap out to *hi*s stepover

ehold facelo*c*k, the

STFU.

Those who think
JOHN CENA
is simply a power
wrestler soon

put the bite on his opponents with his running powerslam finisher, the

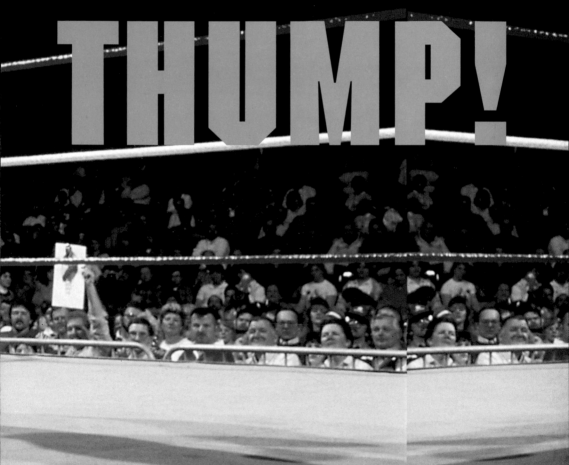

THUMP!

WWE Hall of Famer

JUNK YARD DOG

KANE DOWN
WITH HIS INSATIABLE
"SEX DRIVE"
CHOKEBOMB!

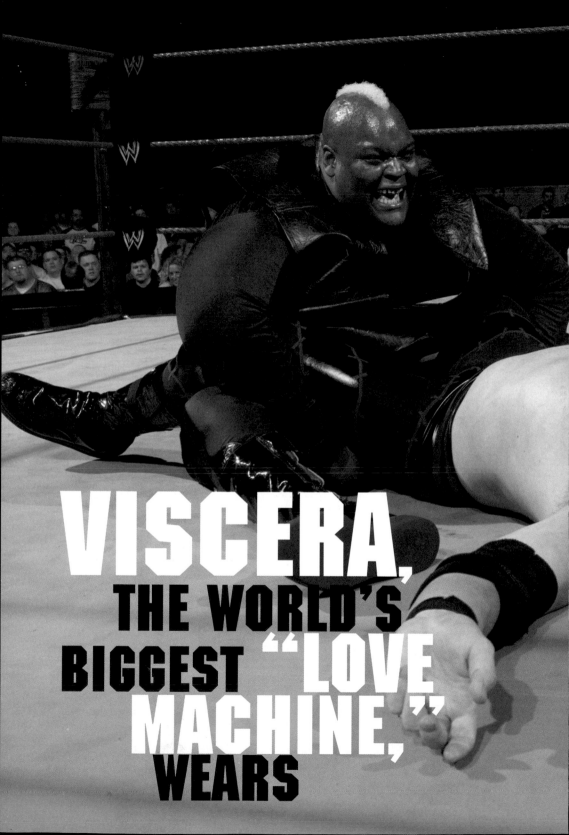

VISCERA, THE WORLD'S BIGGEST "LOVE MACHINE," WEARS

must bow down to the
King of Kings,
TRIPLE H,
and his double
underhook
facebuster, the
PEDIGREE!

Even the legendary
Nature Boy

RIC
FLAIR

PUTTING KANE IN A THREE-QUARTERS FACELOCK, STEVE AUSTIN OPENS UP A CAN OF WHOOP-ASS WITH THE STONE COLD STUNNER!

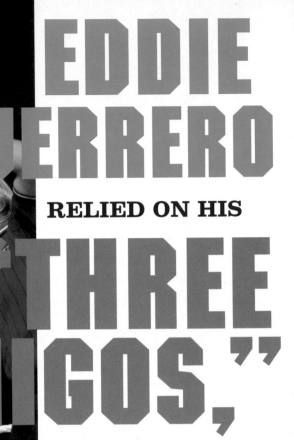

EDDIE GUERRERO

RELIED ON HIS

"THREE AMIGOS,"

A RAPID
SUCCESSION
OF VERTICAL
SUPLEXES, TO
WEAR DOWN
LIGHTNING-FAST
OPPONENTS
LIKE
REY MYSTERIO.

BATISTA GIVES ORLANDO JORDAN THE "THUMBS DOWN," THEN EXPLODES WITH A DEVASTATING BATISTA BOMB TO THE CANVAS!

forcing him to
submit to the
agonizing

CAMEL CLUTCH!

The
IRON SHEIK
rears back on a
chinlocked
Bob Backland,

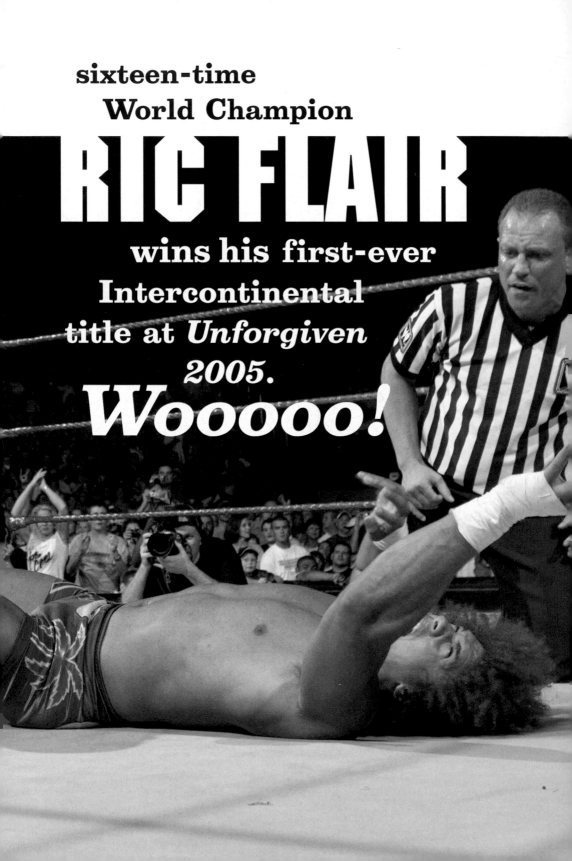

sixteen-time
World Champion
RIC FLAIR
wins his first-ever
Intercontinental
title at *Unforgiven*
2005.
Wooooo!

Wrapping Carlito up in his
FIGURE-FOUR
LEGLOCK,

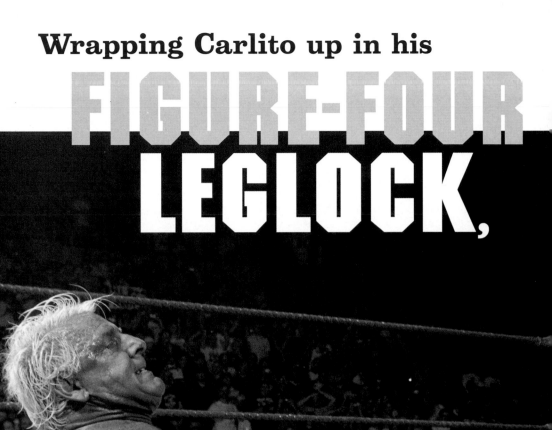

CURT HENNIG—
A.K.A.
MR. PERFECT
—TRANSFORMED
A STANDARD
FISHERMAN'S
SUPLEX AND BRIDGE
INTO HIS PINFALL
FINISHER, THE
PERFECT PLEX.

KURT ANGLE

slaps on the **ANGLE LOCK,** and the **"WRESTLING MACHINE"** won't let go until Undertaker **TAPS OUT!**

a back-to-back
facebuster variation
of his grandfather's
Gory Special.

CHAVO GUERRERO JR.

plants Paul London
with the
GORY
BOMB,

JAKE "THE SNAKE" ROBERTS was pure POISON to his adversaries, as was his DDT, the name of which was derived from the chemical pesticide dichloro-diphenyl-trichloroethane.

NECK, AND PULLS BACK WITH THE **CRIPPLER CROSSFACE!**

CHRIS BENOIT

LOCKS UP CARLITO'S LEFT ARM, CHINLOCKS HIS

SIGNATURE MOVES
TO THE
MAT

POCKET BOOKS, a division of Simon & Schuster, Inc.
1230 Avenue of the Americas, New York, NY 10020

Library of Congress Cataloging-in-Publication Data

McAvennie, Mike.
  Signature moves: the finishing moves of sport entertainment
  superstars/Michael McAvennie.
    p. cm.
  ISBN-13: 978-1-4165-3280-4
  ISBN-10:   1-4165-3280-3
  1. Wrestlers—Pictorial works. 2. Wrestling. I. Title.

GV1196.A1M35 2006
796.812—dc22

                                                    2006049841

This Pocket Books trade paperback edition November 2006

10 9 8 7 6 5 4 3 2 1

Designed by Richard Oriolo

Visit us on the World Wide Web
http://www.simonsays.com
http://www.wwe.com

Manufactured in the United States of America

For information regarding special discounts for bulk purchases,
please contact Simon & Schuster Special Sales at 1-800-456-6798
or business@simonandschuster.com.

SIGNATURE MOVES

MICHAEL McAVENNIE

POCKET BOOKS

NEW YORK   LONDON   TORONTO   SYDNEY